Who are you Monsieur Gurdjieff?

Who are you Monsieur Gurdjieff?

René Zuber

Translated by Jenny Koralek
With a Foreword by P. L. Travers

Routledge & Kegan Paul

LONDON, BOSTON
AND HENLEY

This translation
first published in 1980
by Routledge & Kegan Paul Ltd
39 Store Street,
London WC1E 7DD,
9 Park Street,
Boston, Mass. 02108, USA and
Broadway House,
Newtown Road,
Henley-on-Thames,
Oxon RG9 1EN

Set in 10/12 Linotron 202 Sabon by
Input Typesetting Ltd
London
and printed in Great Britain by
Lowe & Brydone Ltd
Thetford, Norfolk

Translated from Qui êtes-vous Monsieur Gurdjieff?
French edition © René Zuber 1977
English edition © Jenny Koralek 1980

British Library Cataloguing in Publication Data
Zuber, René
    Who are you, Monsieur Gurdjieff?
    1. Gurdjieff, George
    I. Title
    197'.2   B4249.G84   80–40876

    ISBN 0 7100 0674 8

Foreword

The writer René Zuber was by nature a parabolist. It was this that enabled him to record for the ear that lies behind the ear what he himself had been able to perceive with the eye behind the eye.

The subject of his book was also a parabolist, one who communicated what he so significantly had to tell not only through his many-levelled allegorical writings – *All and Everything, Meetings with Remarkable Men*, etc. – but, most equivocal when most candid, by glance, gesture, story, axiom and the communicative silence that is more articulate than words.

It was this bardic element in Gurdjieff, the palpable, earthy, diurnal man, that gave him his air of timelessness, of being a scion of legend rather than of history. Rumour, fable, anecdote accrued to him by natural law as burrs do to the pelt of a fox. Tell the story of his life and inevitably, in spite of names, dates and locality, it will not be biography but saga. In his own idiosyncratic terminology, it will be 'an otherwise'.

Who are you, Mr Gurdjieff? René Zuber may well ask! But his book makes it clear that he is putting the question to himself equally with his subject, letting it lead him not so much to an answer as to further questions of lineage, genealogy, kith. Who are you, Arthur, Taliesin, Prester John, Mullah Nassr

Eddin, St George, Al Khidr, Z'ul Qarnain – you timeless men who weave your way through time, tradition and myth?

Gurdjieff, bright and dark himself, would have been familiar with these heroes in all their colours of the spectrum. Indeed, the last-mentioned, an Islamic honorific – 'He of the Two Horns' – assimilated to the historical Alexander the Great, was, in the teeth of the Koran (Surah XVIII.82), castigated in *All and Everything* as 'that arch-vainglorious Greek'. Gurdjieff, who never said anything unintentionally, would have had a reason for this.

Was it because, as men before and since have done, Alexander set out to conquer the visible world as hero? Or rather that he aimed still higher – to lay siege to the invisible and, without propitiating the tutelary deities, arrogate to himself the name of god? Steeped as he was in ancient lore, would not Gurdjieff, in that pejorative phrase, have been pointing to the enormity of such an enterprise and also to the headlong lapse from its mythological requirements – the attempt to steal the tripod of divination; the fish lost, through inattention, into the two convergent seas; the insensate cutting of the Gordian Knot?

From time beyond time that famous sword-thrust has been hailed as the ultimate solution. Slice it through at a stroke – bravo! But any Old Wife will tell you, without perhaps knowing the why of it, that to cut a knot is unlucky. Gurdjieff would have known the why. Anyone who, as a child, has lain among the woodshavings in his father's workshop and listened to the story of Gilgamesh will certainly have also learned that knots proverbially contain secrets – Solomon's Knot; the Knot as one of the emblems of Buddha; Vishnu's Knot; the Comascene Knot; True Lovers' Knots; the Knots of May; the Knots that bring the sailor home. And secrets need to be unravelled. Cut through them and the meaning is lost. By this reckoning, Alexander would undoubtedly have lost both the world and the meaning.

Parabolically, then, it can be said that Gurdjieff's teaching was itself a kind of unravelling, not so much a discovering as an uncovering of secret things. What had been wound had to be unwound. For those pupils who were capable of following the thread, he unravelled something of what in him and, by reflection, in themselves, had been ravelled. Who am I? Why am I here? What is my purpose? His gnomic oracles, most full of guile when seemingly most innocent, were expressly designed to wake men to this three-fold question; to sound, like Attar and Rumi before him, a stringent reveille to those who fail to ask it.

His trumpet call still reverberates and its portent is still to be assessed. It can be said of him with certainty, however, that he did not cease from mental fight, nor did his sword sleep in his hand. As to what he built of Jerusalem, this will be witnessed to, fallibly – as all eternal principles are witnessed to – by the fallible children of time.

René Zuber's fresh, vivid, wholly unprejudiced testimony shows him to be a perceptive and veracious member of this tribe.

P. L. Travers

Acknowledgments

Mme Zuber wishes to thank Annette Courtenay-Mayers, Natasha Jobst, Jenny Koralek and Verena Keable for their assistance in the translation of her husband's book.

Who are you
Monsieur Gurdjieff?

Who are you
Monsieur Gurdjieff?

I was first taken to Mr Gurdjieff's flat at a time very different from the present.

Paris during the war, under German occupation, was in the grip of the blackout: if the slightest ray of light filtered through a window it had to be smothered quickly and the curtains more tightly drawn. The city was under curfew: no one would have dared, on pain of death, to go out into the deserted streets after eleven o'clock at night. It was the reign of what we called the 'restrictions', that is to say, of organized poverty, with its corollary, obsession with food; not to mention the constant hammering of Nazi propaganda which tried, in vain, to rob the Parisians of their last glimmer of hope.

We were quite cut off from the rest of the world. No wonder I had not heard of Gurdjieff's American pupils, though they were very close to his heart. As for the vast country of Russia, all we knew of it was what we learnt from his family (so he did have a family like everybody else) and through a few old friends who clung to him 'like parasites' and who from time to time turned up at his table or in his kitchen. He behaved towards them, it seemed to me, with generous and good-natured tyranny, in contrast to the way he treated us, his pupils, on whom he made other demands.

Who was he? I feel sure that many of those who approached him, if not all, were tempted to ask him this question; but such was his prestige, such was his power, that they never dared to ask him outright.

Some people were simply curious, others had an inner thirst and had been told that here was a spring at which this thirst could be quenched. The shock of the encounter, however, always exceeded the expectation and some preferred to run away rather than undergo an experience that might well force them to put in question all their accepted ideas.

When I knew him, in 1943, he was no longer young: he was sixty-five years old.[1] He had both the majesty of an old man and the agility of a fencer capable of delivering a lightning thrust; no matter how unpredictable his changes of mood, however surprising his manifestations, his impressive calm never deserted him.

'He looks like Bodhidarma', Philippe Lavastine had told me before taking me to see him, 'because he has the sternness of an awakener of conscience, and because of his large moustaches.'[2]

I thought he had, if anything, a reassuring air, like a Macedonian smuggler or an old Cretan *capetan*.[3] He had that kind of authority. He would have been quite capable of throwing you into the River Seine – having first relieved you of your watch and wallet – and then of extending a helping hand to fish you out again. Oddly enough, on being rescued, you would have felt the need to thank him.

The word 'authority' has many connotations, however, and may lead to misunderstandings. Let us say
that there emanated from Mr Gurdjieff such an
impression of quiet strength that even animals sensed
it. It is said that dogs and cats followed him in the
street. I never actually witnessed such an event, but
I often saw people who could have been taken for
wolves become so tame that they would end up eating out of his hand.

His gait and his gestures were never hurried, but
flowed in unison with the rhythm of his breathing
like those of a peasant or a mountaineer.

I remember the day when I arrived late for an
appointment that he had given me. I galloped down
the Avenue Carnot, bounded up his stairs four at a
time, and started to stammer an excuse. But he simply let fall two words: 'Never hurry.' Was all this
because he had met many human beings during his
life and knew their every weakness, and because the
human condition was for him an almost constant
subject of meditation; or was there another reason?
He seemed to be filled with an experience – almost
incommunicable – which set him at an unbearable
distance from the common run of mortals.

If there existed a certain connivance between him
and you, stretched like a narrow bridge over the
abyss, it rested on such direct perceptions as *cold,
hot, height, width, yesterday, today, tomorrow, I,
here, now*, rather than on intellectual speculations.
It was a hidden understanding which had a taste of

sincerity anchored in the innermost depths of one's being.

Paul Valéry, in his essay on Leonardo da Vinci, says: 'What a man leaves behind him are the dreams inspired by his *name* and by the *works* that make his name a symbol of admiration, hate or indifference.'

All we can do, according to Valéry, is 'to imagine such a man' and, he adds, 'if this man excels in all fields the effort to perceive him in his wholeness is all the greater.'[4]

So it remains for those now living to bring Gurdjieff to life through what he has given his name to, that is to say, the books he wrote, as well as what was accomplished in other fields under his direction and inspiration. For it is always necessary to go back to the source. Each generation after ours will engage in a new reading of Gurdjieff with material of its own.

Those of us who knew him will not go looking for him in any archives, whether printed or of the institutional kind, in the hope of recapturing an echo of his voice. We will call upon our personal experience, our own most vivid memories.

How can we think of Gurdjieff? As a musician? Choreographer? Writer? Physician? Psychiatrist? Master cook?

'The only absolutely free man, if such a man could

be conceived of, would be the man in whom not a single gesture smacked of imitation.'[5]

Let me begin by describing his utter contempt for social conventions. He would have seated a Nobel prize winner next to a roadsweeper, a 'lady' next to a prostitute.

This being so, it is all the more surprising that he could deal so harshly with one particular category of people who, after all, earn their living like anybody else, namely, journalists. He always kept them at bay and would not allow them to cross his door.

One day I was present when the following scene took place. Two young men had had the nerve to force their way in and, presenting their press cards, declared that they were on the editorial staff of a well-known newspaper. Someone went to announce them to Mr Gurdjieff but, before they had even had time to take three steps into the hall, he appeared in person and chased them out as if they were vermin.

That he braved the power of the press on every occasion is one thing. But on top of that, when his pupils went to the trouble of bringing a world-famous personality to him, expecting such an encounter to result in some kind of mutual recognition at least, more often than not things would turn out contrary to their wishes. After a fairly good start the important holder of the Légion d'Honneur would suddenly feel himself in a situation which no longer tallied with his idea of himself. He would get out of his depth and go to pieces.

5

Perhaps people only go to bullfights in the hope of seeing the matador, after a number of passes, destroy his adversary in a single blow – or be killed himself. I myself do not go looking for this kind of spectacle. I used to wonder what would have happened if Stendhal, Baudelaire or Proust had been seated at his table. Would he have mistaken one of them for any old pen-pusher? I found it painful to ask myself such questions. I preferred to say to myself: 'Poor man! He is insensitive to the niceties of the French language. He may be a connoisseur of Russian vodka, but he doesn't know a thing about French wines!'

In this I was mistaken. Gurdjieff always played a role in front of newcomers, a role which varied according to the circumstances. If the newcomer was a prominent person, and if, in the interests of his own people, he had to be careful not to offend him, he could get him where he wanted him in the twinkling of an eye. At other times he was seen to ignore even the most obvious qualities of the newcomer to the point of appearing stupid. He did not care how bad an opinion the victim might later have of him. If the other had seen nothing, understood nothing, then let him go to the devil!

For at the same time he was playing a role, to him a much more important one, for the benefit of his pupils. This role was designed to show us what the essential reality of any man amounts to, in spite of appearances. If good-natured souls like myself could not bear such a sight – never mind! One does not become adult without undergoing such trials.

Mr Gurdjieff's most remarkable feature was the way he looked at you. From the very first meeting you felt that he could see right through you. You had the impression that you had been *seen* and that he knew you far better than you knew yourself.

It was an extraordinary feeling.

Like many disillusioned idealists, I had finally accepted that human communication can be nothing more than 'the deaf talking to the deaf' (though I wonder whether the word 'blind' would not be even more suitable for this condition of mutual ignorance). So, at the age of forty, perhaps halfway through my life, the possibility of at last being known opened up before me a dazzling hope.

At the same time I felt, but in a very confused way, that there would be a price to pay for this. I had been told that to frequent the company of a man like Gurdjieff could be very dangerous. But after all, what had I to fear? A taste for risk exists, thank God, deep in the heart of every son of Adam. Money to pay? I had none. Sweat to pour? I was still young enough to believe myself endowed with limitless strength. Illusions to lose? Having gone from disappointment to disappointment, I had already, I believed, lost them all. Prejudices to overcome? A man like me does not have any!

I was boasting like this as I entered his flat, like

the long-distance swimmer who, having strained himself to the utmost, at the risk of his life, at last feels firm ground under his feet. Half-suffocated, yet he smiles as he shakes the water from his nose, mouth and ears. The old fighter had perceived it all at a glance. And he had seen or felt many other things besides: my shortcomings, my weaknesses, my fears.

It was then that he gave me a nickname, which made me feel that I had been accepted into the circle of his pupils. Each of them, as I was to discover later, was endowed with a nickname, often very funny and more descriptive than his real name. One of us, a slender girl, was called 'Maigriche'. Another, a delicious creature, was called 'Brioche', later, 'ex-Brioche'. A professor was simply called 'Maître', an American lady, 'Crocodile', hinting at crocodile tears. I myself became 'Demi-Petit'. For a long time this name remained an enigma, even a provocation for me. 'Petit', granted, since I am tall, but why 'Demi'? Why not just ask him? It was not so simple. He gave me a chance one day, roguishly saying in front of several people: 'With Demi-Petit all things really very, very good. Except one thing . . .' He was waiting for me to say: 'Which thing, Mr Gurdjieff?' But I had seen it coming. So I settled into cowardly silence, as if I had not understood the magnificent opportunity he had offered me. I also fixed a particular kind of smile on my face which did not fool him for a moment, but which would perhaps make the others believe that I was acting in connivance with him, and had understood it all. He did not persist. Some time later, in a totally different way, he managed to convey to me very well what he had tried to tell me that day.

When Mr Gurdjieff was nearby it was impossible to sleep in peace. Nobody was safe from being tripped up and sent flying. It is a wonder that there were not more broken bones. His table, at the end of a meal, when a great silence fell to make way for the questions of his pupils, resembled the mat in a judo club. The master, his head shaven like that of a samurai, waited calmly without moving. The 'Monsieur, may I ask you a question?' that broke the silence was something of a ritual, comparable with the salutation of two *judokas* bowing deeply to each other. At that moment the respect that filled the room reached its peak.

I knew what it was to be beyond good and evil, beyond fear, the first time I asked Mr Gurdjieff a question. I said to him: 'Monsieur, in order to search for truth one has to run the risk of making mistakes. Now, I am afraid of making mistakes, so I remain sitting at my window and I see no reason why it should ever end. . . .'

I had put this question into words because Philippe, who was sitting on my left, had nudged me and whispered: 'Go on! Now's your chance!', because Mr Gurdjieff had granted me an 'oï, oï' of approval; because all eyes were turned towards me, and I found myself suddenly confronted by infinite space, just as I imagine an astronaut, in a state of weightlessness, would if he opened the door of his capsule. In the split second of silence that followed I felt all the familiar currents of life flowing into me again with such force that I would not even have heard Mr Gurdjieff's answer had it been other than it was.

This answer rolled over me, into me, like an avalanche. I heard a voice as though through a fog, coming from the mountain, affirming that yes, it was indeed so, I was not good for much – a good-for-nothing – 'a piece of live meat', 'a shit'. 'In my own country', Gurdjieff went on, 'you even pay people to get rid of it.' I could not be relied upon. I might have a cheque book in my pocket, but my signature was worthless. However, if I wished, it could all change. Later on, perhaps at the end of the war, my signature would be worth something.

To my insidious question: 'Monsieur, who are you, then? Are you a true master or a false one? I never board a ship without being perfectly sure of the length of the journey and the identity of the captain' – to this question he gave me no answer.

He had thrown me back onto myself. 'And *you*, who are *you*, then?' – with such force that I shall never forget it.

It was a master stroke.

Some time after that particular evening I rang his

doorbell one morning, because I had been entrusted with an errand for him. There was a shuffling of slippers in the hall; then the door opened. Mr Gurdjieff seemed surprised to see me. He beckoned me into the kitchen where he was busying himself. At this early hour of the morning the flat was still empty. I was about to explain the reason for my visit and give him the small package I had brought, when he said: 'I am short of money to go to the cinema this afternoon. You twenty francs? Lend me.' I was dumbfounded! What? Give money to him, to an all-powerful patriarch who had so often feasted us at his table! Why, only the night before a good thirty of us had been his guests. He must need money very badly to make such a request to *me*. And, indeed, did I even have enough money on me?

I hid my confusion (probably very badly), fumbled in all my pockets, drew out a banknote which I handed him, together with the package.

Then, as quickly as possible, I left, without asking him to settle up with me for the errand.

He had the art of taking you by surprise in deep sleep. Now and then he would break off in the middle of a sentence to ask someone point blank: 'What's half a hundred?'

Only the person he was speaking to would understand, and even then not always, why he was being thus singled out.

Once, at his table, I was called back to myself by

11

a perfectly ordinary remark while digesting my meal, pleasantly warm, and filled with a sense of well-being as I admired his astonishing play-acting. I was sitting next to Louise Le Prudhomme, an old Breton woman who was one of the most faithful of the faithful. Even though she limped she always arrived on time, wearing her flat-heeled shoes and carrying the umbrella she used as a walking-stick. In the past she had been a militant unionist and had spent her life working in public hospitals in contact with all the world's suffering. And now, there she was, a testimony to the presence of ordinary French people at Mr Gurdjieff's table.

We were squashed tightly together, elbows touching, dishes overlapping, while other guests, standing behind us, had to put their plates on top of the piano. All eyes were turned towards Mr Gurdjieff seated on his much-loved old divan. We forgot the discomfort of our surroundings. We even forgot where we were because the spectacle which followed the various toasts drunk to 'the idiots' was extraordinary.

Interrupting his act in a pause so brief that I believe no one even noticed, Gurdjieff flung at me: 'You impudent person! Look! You in Mlle Le Prudhomme's way.'

It was so true that I sat up at once.

It could be asked whether it is useful to recall such a slight anecdote. Yes, without doubt it is. Such moments are invaluable. For in them one sees Gurdjieff letting his arrow fly at the right moment and in the right place, *having taken all the circumstances into account.*

My feeling for Mlle Le Prudhomme had been alive when we sat down at the table, but Gurdjieff had seen it fade as soon as my attention was taken by the food and vanish the moment I had allowed myself to drift into contented admiration, like a cow settling down in her stall.

It was at this very moment that he *called me back to myself*, making me aware of my absence.

Another surprise for me was the discovery of Mr Gurdjieff's dealings with His Majesty Money. He talked about it with a freedom bordering on cynicism.

Is this how one imagines a spiritual guide? The first time I saw him counting a bundle of notes with all the dexterity of a cashier, it was something of a shock.

As a child I had been told: if someone close to you gives you money, never check the number of notes in front of him, 'It's bad manners.' This was one of the few rules of conduct engrained in me. Of course Mr Gurdjieff transgressed all these rules which express a kind of social hypocrisy rather than true delicacy of feeling.

I was irritated by the discreet pressure exercised by the 'secretary' of the group in the matter of the ever-recurring 'material question' – I could even say I was scandalized, to the point where one day I spoke up:

'Monsieur? May I ask you a question? You ask us for money. Why?' At this, certain people turned towards me and looked at me with horror. But I went on because it was too late to draw back. 'No doubt,' I said, 'you want us to understand something by this, but what?'

Mr Gurdjieff sized me up in one glance. 'You free Thursday? Right! Then come and have lunch with me. We'll have real coffee and I'll explain to you. . . .' (In those days our only drink was a revolting concoction of roasted barley. Real coffee was a treat in itself!)

After lunch I followed Mr Gurdjieff into the little room which was always kept for private conversations. It was like being in a peaceful library, the walls of which would, anywhere else, have been covered with old leatherbound books. In fact, it was not rare manuscripts that lined the shelves, but jars containing spices from all over the world in the form of bulbs, leaves or roots.

Today I cannot remember exactly the conversation that took place over our cups of Turkish coffee. What emerged from it was that Mr Gurdjieff had a big family and that this big family cost him a lot of money.

I could not help feeling, in some strange way, that he was not being completely sincere. I was still waiting for the word that would give me a glimpse of the deep reason, the esoteric reason for his demands for money.

Some time later I was invited to come and see Mr Gurdjieff. He asked me if I could do an errand for him in a remote district of Paris. Of course I could! He then gave me a piece of paper, yellow with age, a receipt from a pawnbroker, and enough money to redeem the object pawned by him a long time before. It was then that I began to suspect the reality of his financial difficulties.

Off I went, and after the usual formalities, the object was handed over to me. It was a big gold watch, with a chain of heavy links also made of gold. It reminded me of my father's watch. From the lustre of the metal alone one could tell that it had been the companion of a lifetime. As I felt the weight of this object in the palm of my hand I glimpsed in a flash a whole side of Mr Gurdjieff's life which I had up till then obstinately failed to recognize. I was indeed ashamed of myself.

Even though I had doubts about Mr Gurdjieff, since I understood nothing of his deep intention, I never ceased to admire the assurance with which he made his way through all kinds of complications, *which he had often provoked himself.* How many times have I seen him calmly walking through a minefield which he was either defusing or, on the contrary, exploding with all the skill of an expert.

I think I understand now why he rebuked journalists and other manipulators of public opinion (and, indeed, his pupils too when we discussed affairs of state or the fate of the world, at the end of a good meal). It was for their failure to take responsibility for their actions and for their lack of conscience. Journalists are like the cells of a nerve. They transmit information at top speed, without always being able to verify its accuracy, and without ever foreseeing the short- or the long-term effect of the news thus transmitted.

At Mr Gurdjieff's side I learnt that the saying 'Only the truth wounds', has its complement: 'Only the truth heals.'

The moment one sees who is in front of one – and he saw your past, present and future – what cannot be dared?

The one who sees nothing will always wound.

If I had to sum up in a word everything I understood about Mr Gurdjieff I would say that, compared with the behaviour of any of us, or of my family, or of anyone I came across in public, he was a monster of *modesty*.

People have said that he was cynical, coarse, and that he told jokes which would make a regiment blush. There is a host of anecdotes to support this view, some of them extremely spicy, and on the basis of these he could be described as a monster of immorality.

In reality, however, everyone who approached him saw only one side of him. Like a very high mountain, he was not to be discovered in his entirety. Many are those who have answered, in one way or another, the call of the mountain. Some among them had the idea of drawing closer to him in order to understand better from where his greatness came. But when one is too close one can see nothing any more. So, without further ado, it is necessary to attempt the climb, that is to say, to measure oneself, inch by inch, against the reality of each slope.

We addressed him very simply, calling him 'Monsieur' or 'Monsieur Gurdjieff'. I had noticed, however, that members of his family and, in general, all those who had known him in Russia, called him, with affectionate familiarity not 'Monsieur Gurdjieff' but 'Gurgivantch'. One day I tried to imitate them, hoping that this would enable me – at little cost – to join this intimate circle. But I was immediately put in my place in such a way that I never wanted to do it again. I learnt something about him that day, but at my own expense.

I remember another lesson he gave me at his table, during the toasts, before I put that question to him which caused me to be called 'piece of live meat'. My glass had already been filled with armagnac several times – one for each toast. As I was not used to drinking so much alcohol I was cheating, keeping my glass half full in order to empty it at the last possible moment. Mr Gurdjieff noticed this: '*One must not drink with food in mouth. Because alcohol noble; wants to be alone on palate.*'

Addressing my neighbour a moment later he said: '*Director! Always do only one thing at a time, that*

of the present moment. But do it well, be in it en-
tirely. . . . Too bad if meanwhile business worth
many millions waits at the door. . . . Man is always
doing seven things at once; if he does as I say, even
for one little thing, the other six will look after
themselves.'

I do not know if this advice was meant for me too,
but anyway I heard it and profited from it. I discovered that when he wanted one of us to understand
something important he often addressed himself to
someone else. He knew both how to disturb one's
self-esteem and how to lull it with cunning and delicacy. For Mr Gudjieff was a master of artifice. One
could also say: a master costumier. For truth cannot
walk naked in the street but must wear borrowed
clothing so that we can bear to look it in the face.
Somewhere he speaks of himself as 'A Teacher of
Dancing'.

To be honest, I must admit that a kind of fear
lurked somewhere in me, a fear of joining in the
dance with the whole of myself, a fear of the unknown. It was of this fear that I had spoken to him
in veiled words when we first crossed swords.

Where did this man come from, this man who
seemed to have given himself the task of interrupting
our sleep and waking us up? He had this power. But
in whose name did he exercise it? And to what end?

Had he given us the slightest indication that would
have allowed us to put him into any historical category already known to us – whether philosophical,

ethical or religious – I would probably have gone to sleep, reassured. For we Westerners need dictionaries and encyclopedias to satisfy our insatiable need to know *by always bringing back the unknown to the known*. We may believe that we are free from all prejudices and from the influences of our time, but we do not remain any the less attached to the way of thinking which has been inculcated into us since childhood: we proceed from definitions. That is what we call 'liking clear ideas'. But by dint of accumulating definitions we end up 'by knowing everything and understanding nothing'.[6] Remember the African's tragic cry: 'White men think too much.'

If I now open the Petit Robert of proper nouns, or any other dictionary or encyclopedia, I will not find the name of GURDJIEFF (George Ivanovitch). Perhaps I should rejoice over this fact rather than deplore it.

Mr Gurdjieff always found a way of making himself understood, even though he ignored the grammatical rules of the many languages he spoke. He was very cavalier in his treatment of these languages: for example, he would intermingle Russian and Greek words with French and English, all admirably chosen for their effectiveness.

It is not his ignorance of syntax that I want to emphasize here – which might anyway only have been feigned, since he was quick to catch the slightest nuance of what was said to him – but rather his intense interest in words. How many discussions

19

were needed, for example, in order to determine the difference between 'sentir' and 'ressentir', or between 'détendre' and 'relâcher'! These discussions, which would suddenly start up with one or other of us, and in which he made sure he himself always had the last word, were, I think, a kind of relaxation for him. He was intrigued by the colourful expressions and the slang used by the man in the street, whereas what he called 'bon ton langage' bored him.

I remember he asked me once (it was in the early days): 'What you do in life, Demi-Petit?' I was making short documentary films of which I was the 'director'. But the term seemed a little too pompous to dare use in front of him. The simpler and more accurate expression 'producer' was then coming into use, but I was afraid he would not understand it. So I told him I 'created' documentary films. 'Create?' It was as if I had uttered some appalling obscenity. 'You not create. You shit!' He enlarged on the theme, which reminds me of the answer given to me in Mosul by a Muslim of exemplary piety and charity. I had been introduced to him by his son who worked in the laboratories of the Iraq Petroleum Company and was therefore already contaminated by Western ideas. Through the son I asked the old man why, in Islam, it is improper to take photographs of men or women. 'Because', he replied, 'on the Day of Judgment you will be asked to give a soul to your pictures, and you will not be able to do it. God alone has the power to create.'

It was in the year 223 after the creation of the World, by objective time calculation, or, as it would be said here on the 'Earth', in the year 1921 after the birth of Christ.

Through the Universe flew the ship Karnak. . . .

on the said 'transspace' ship was Beelzebub with his kinsmen and near attendants. . . .

A newcomer arriving in Mr Gurdjieff's flat in the middle of a series of readings of *Beelzebub's Tales to His Grandson*, had to catch this interplanetary space-ship in mid-air or meet it wherever it had pleased Beelzebub to moor it.

The travellers on this immense journey across time, space and the successive civilizations of our planet, could have found themselves in any part of our solar system. I had the good fortune to come across them *in Tibet* where their little caravan seemed to be up against all sorts of difficulties.

My friends just had time to warn me: 'You'll see. It is not at all what you expect. There will be a lot of strange words which will seem incomprehensible to you. You must know, for instance, that the expression "three-brained beings" means men.'

Around their camps at night these 'three-brained beings' were lighting big fires to protect themselves and their quadruped workers from other 'two-brained beings' which were called 'lions', 'tigers' and 'hyenas'.

21

I was immediately captivated by the charm of this tale, but when it came to the physics of the globe, I think it was, and of earthquakes as 'planetary tremors', I rather lost my bearings.

Carried away by the process of reading aloud, the reader had put too much seriousness into the fact that from the top of the mountains of Tibet, with a good 'Teskooano', one could almost see clearly the opposite side of the earth. (There was no need to turn to a dictionary to understand the word 'Teskooano'!)

My mind was still relatively fresh, however, when we started on a horrible tale. It told of the unfortunate followers of a sect, 'the Self-Tamers', who allowed themselves to die, immured in small cells through whose tiny apertures bread and water were passed to them, with great reverence, every twenty-four hours.

This story made an unforgettable impression on me, so much so that when it came to the question of the planet Mars, of bread, of wheat, and of the process by which everything that exists in the world is linked with everything else, I let myself be lulled for a moment by the words. The author felt an obvious tenderness when speaking of the Earth, that *'long and vain-suffering planet'*, with its vast expanse of water which he called by a strange name in which I recognized, as though discovering it for the first time, the ocean.

The chapter came to an end and I thought that the

reader would now stop. But, imperturbably, he started again:

'Chapter 23, The Fourth Personal Sojourn of Beelzebub on the planet Earth.'

And now new characters appeared: a certain Gornahoor Harhharkh, whose name rang oddly in my ears and who was said to be the 'essence friend' of Beelzebub; there was also the director of an observatory on the planet Mars, whom the author, confused in my mind with Beelzebub, called 'my uncle Tooilan'. I noted in passing that the Teskooano of this uncle enlarged up to 7,285,000 times the visibility of remote cosmic concentrations.

We listened with the greatest seriousness, careful not to yield too quickly to fatigue. I felt it necessary to adapt to the text at each moment. For example, not to try at all costs to grasp the meaning of something that was said only in jest. 'Slow and steady wins the race.' But how was one to tell the difference?

Then came the famous passage about the apes. I learnt that, contrary to the generally accepted idea, rooted in me since childhood, that man is descended from the apes, it is the apes who are descended from man – or, more accurately, from woman. This was because, in the remote past, after the catastrophe of Atlantis had wiped out the men, the unhappy women, deprived of their partners, mated with animals. According to the text, 'they blended their "Exioëhary" with that of various quadruped beings'

23

and from this blending arose the various species of apes.

It was a 'tall story', as the saying goes, but told with such good humour, and mixed with such profound explanations on the duality of the sexes that I asked myself: 'Is this said in jest and if so, to what end? Is it a sort of provocation, or just the pure and simple truth, the "historical" truth?'

I still cannot claim to have clarified entirely this thorny question. It seems, in the light of the most recent anthropological discoveries, that *homo sapiens* has a much more ancient origin than was thought to be the case a few years ago, and that the famous 'link' has not yet been found which would prove that, in fact, man is descended from the ape.

In the course of subsequent readings, I was often led to ask myself equally embarrassing questions about physics, biology, astronomy, medicine and ethnology, for the charm of *Beelzebub's Tales* lies in the fact that one can find absolutely everything in them; 'even the recipe for bortsch', as Mr Gurdjieff would have said.

About the end of the chapter which I heard that evening, I can say little. Due to the heat and to sitting still for so long, I fell asleep, lulled by the monotonous voice of the reader.

I think we had arrived at the capital of the future Egypt, the city of Thebes, when I woke with a start. We were being called to 'make the chain' between the kitchen and the dining room.

Twice during this long endurance test the door had opened to let Mr Gurdjieff pass through. He had sat down among us for a few moments, without interrupting the reader, and had then returned to keep an eye on his stove. Each time the door opened, delicious smells wafted from the kitchen.

'Making the chain' consisted in passing the plates from one person to another, empty on their way out, laden on their way back. It was a simple movement which, at ten o'clock at night, after two hours of immobility, was deeply satisfying. With all distinctions as to age, size and sex abolished, the chain, when formed, functioned as a whole. At one end, Mr Gurdjieff took the dishes from the oven, carved the meat or poultry, and, with supreme authority, shared out the helpings. At the other end, the food was kept warm on plates covered by soup bowls. When this ballet was over the circle would close around the table, and together we would eat the extraordinary fare Mr Gurdjieff had prepared for us.

I have lingered a little over this description because the distance from kitchen to dining room – which might suggest to some people that from production to consumption – suggested to me that great chain which exists everywhere in the universe between substances (or energies) of different levels. For Beelzebub the entire universe, from the atom to the most distant galaxies, consists of an immense process of mutual feeding which he called *Iraniranumange*.

Mr Gurdjieff excelled in the art of cooking as well

as in the arts of music and dance (or rhythm). I will not risk going into matters about which I am not especially competent to speak, although in this I do not show myself a good disciple of the master. Many anecdotes illustrate that he often, for reasons best known to himself, enjoyed putting the financier in the painter's place and the painter in the place of the financier. It is one of his peculiarities which has been least understood.

In a society like ours, obsessed with efficiency, the word specialization is no laughing matter. (This is why real physicians are becoming so rare.) As a matter of fact Mr Gurdjieff excelled in medicine. He also cooked like a gourmet with the knowledge of a scientist. 'That, special Georgian dish, little chicken, rice and onion, must eat with fingers', he would say. 'That, Kurdish dessert; when suitor proposes and has been accepted, next day he sends this dish to future bride.' He cooked scientifically, like a dietician who foresees the action on the organism of each dish, each flavouring, each spice.

One day I ventured a remark on this subject. 'In fact, Monsieur, cooking could well be a branch of medicine?' which brought the response, 'No, medicine branch of cooking.'

It was wartime, or just after the war. The business of shopping for food had become the general preoccupation of the French; to eat their fill their immediate concern. Often, between two overnight journeys (and in what conditions!) one of us would

go to fetch poultry for the table in the rue des Colonels-Renard; another, who could have taught a
professional butcher a thing or two, waited before
dawn on the cold stone floor of Les Halles to make
a fruitful deal.

Eating is the sacred act by which we absorb and
assimilate what Gurdjieff called 'the first food'.[7]

This act asks for our appreciation. It has the value
of a call to order since it brings us into communion
with the natural forces *which we constantly forget
we depend upon*. It cannot be done in the way one
gives swill to a pig, while the mind and feelings are
given over to their own affairs or dreams.

This is why the meals at Mr Gurdjieff's table always began in silence and the dialogues – questions
and answers, that so often resembled a tournament
in the lists – were kept for the end.

I do not know how to sum up the highly varied
impressions we experienced during these dinners.
Today, if I ask myself this question, I would speak
of a *recaptured childhood*: I was finding once more
the taste of my own childhood, which had been in-
terrupted by life. Indeed, I was becoming a child
again instead of the elderly young man I had become
– a child who was not interested in the past, but was
filled with wonder and astonishment at the present,
which assailed him from all sides. The strong organic
sensations in the gut and in the taste buds which
belong to childhood, and which are fundamental to
the future development of a human being, remain in

my memory as the *basso ostinato* of all conversations with Mr Gurdjieff.

At night, back at the hotel room where I was then staying, I made notes on the events I had lived through during the course of the day. My notes soon turned into questions which I put to myself. But they disappeared completely when I had understood and dated the note I now find in one of my diaries: 'Wednesday 25 July 1945: it is more necessary for me to *work* than to take notes.'

I must point out, that in Gurdjieff's language, doing an inner exercise, meditating, practising yoga, etc., was simply called 'working', which was a shortened way of saying 'working on oneself'.

If one doubted Gurdjieff's genius, evidence of it could be found here. Of all the values of our civilization, the only one which remained intact (in those days) was the value attached to work.

It is important to point out that we did not then possess any written account of Gurdjieff's system of ideas. *In Search of the Miraculous* by P. D. Ouspensky had not yet been published. I thought that by writing I could keep track of the moment which had just been lived through, and I hoped that by gathering all the little pieces together I would one day see the outline of the *Gurdjieff continent* taking shape before my eyes like a huge jigsaw puzzle.

Ouspensky did just this in fact, and he did it in a masterly way. I possessed neither his intellectual capacity, nor his drive, nor his *professionalism*.

28

Since this word 'professionalism' has come to mind, let me pay tribute to Ouspensky by recounting a conversation at which I happened to be present.

Someone had brought Mr Gurdjieff the manuscript of *In Search of the Miraculous* in its English version, which was going to be published first; Mr Gurdjieff had had time to look at it and to approve it. Asked what he thought of Ouspensky, he answered: 'Ouspensky? Yes, he good journalist.' This terse judgment astonished me, because Ouspensky had been at Gurdjieff's side for seven years. He had then left him to teach in London independently and, years later, posthumously, arranged to have sent to Gurdjieff this admirable, exact and faithful testimony.

Gurdjieff's appreciation will not be understood and will be considered disdainful unless one restores to the word 'journalist' its true *'professional'* meaning.

I offer the above anecdote to my re-instated journalist friends.

Mr Gurdjieff, for us, was like another world, a world apart from our friends and families. In what way, with what words could I have spoken of all that I experienced in his presence to anybody, even to my own mother? One day, however, against my will I had to give in to Mr Gurdjieff's insistence that I bring my old mother to lunch with him.

When she was seated at his table, with a dozen other people, whom I knew only slightly, I am not sure which was stronger in me, curiosity or fear. At that time she was still remarkably active. Since she devoted herself unstintingly to all the humble and unfortunate folk who crossed her path, she was considered by some people to be rather odd, whereas others took her for a saint. The most important thing for her was never to be deterred by public opinion. With age she had acquired considerable audacity.

I was sure she would appreciate the comical side of this meeting, and also that she would not be able to prevent herself from coming rashly to the fore. She was deeply puritanical, hated all alcohol, she could not eat spicy food and *risqué* stories made her uneasy.

The fear which I felt for her at that moment was truly filial emotion. I would like to have cast over her shoulders the mantle of Noah himself.

'I love him, says God, who loves his parents. And you know why? Because he who loves his parents, he builds for them a room in heaven and when parents die, room empty, God enters it.'

Things went as I had foreseen, the only difference being that at the beginning of the meal I saw her quietly keeping herself to herself. I kept an eye on her glass. The drink Mr Gurdjieff had offered her, and which she had finally accepted without too much ado, she swallowed in a gulp, as though it were poison. At one point Mr Gurdjieff asked her: 'How many children have you, Mother?' 'I have twenty-seven,' she replied, and began to tell him about those twenty-seven poor fellows just out of the prison at Poissy who she was sheltering in her home. Mr Gurdjieff did not give her time to continue, but proceeded to confide to her that, for his part, he had 'seventy-five wives', a declaration from which she never recovered.

The next day, my mother, back home in Poissy, telephoned me to say that she had been ill all night, that it was the fault of the alcohol she had drunk with 'my old gentleman', and that having thrown up the whole meal she now felt better.

I think neither of us ever mentioned 6 rue des Colonels-Renard again. As for Mr Gurdjieff, he later brought it up with me and said: 'Your mother? Last time: guest. Next time: pupil.' My love for her did not go as far as wishing to throw her into that fiery furnace!

My repeated promises to myself that I would stop writing about our *work* have never been completely kept.

One day I made a note of a thought that had just struck me: '*This teaching is a virile version of the Gospels.*'

What was the date of this note? I do not know. It was certainly written before we had *In Search of the Miraculous*, or any of Mr Gurdjieff's own books.[8] Otherwise we would have been able to verify that he in fact defined his teaching as 'Christian esotericism'.

But this is not how it was presented to us. Is it

necessary to recall here that Gurdjieff's teaching was purely oral, and that it sprang spontaneously out of life circumstances or from dialogues with his pupils? I can vouch for the fact that, during the years I knew him (and this reservation is important), I never heard him 'lecture'. The very idea of seeing him on a lecture platform, or preaching in a pulpit seems absurd to me.

It is true that he never travelled, in France or elsewhere, without a retinue – namely, the motley band of pupils who always astonished hotel managements and the police. They probably did not realize that in antiquity, and even nowadays in Africa and Asia, a master lives in this way, at his pupils' expense, while the pupils live under the watchful eye of the master.

As soon as the idea flashed across my mind, that the teaching was none other than a version of the Gospels in different language, I was overcome with great joy and at the same time a certain anxiety. Why? To put it simply, let us say that I had a feeling of stepping into private territory. For Christianity was not born yesterday. It belongs by right to the saints and elders of the Church. Furthermore, although nowadays its precepts are universally doubted, it is clearly still the foundation of our institutions, codes and ethics and our thought is steeped in it. Could it really be that until now we had not recognized it in this unknown teaching?

In order to recognize it in a form we had never

seen before we would have had to have tasted its
essence (which keeps its flavour throughout all
changes of appearance). The essence of Christianity?
Do not expect me to try to define what appears to
be beyond definition. It would, however, be wrong
to pretend to know nothing about it.

When I open the Gospels I receive a very strong
impact. They burn with words of such piercing
intelligence that they can never be forgotten:

> And why beholdest thou the mote that is in thy
> brother's eye, but considerest not the beam that
> is in thine own eye? (Matthew 7:3)

> This they said, tempting him, that they might
> have to accuse him. But Jesus stooped down,
> and with his finger wrote on the ground, as
> though he heard them not. So when they con-
> tinued asking him, he lifted up himself, and
> said unto them, He that is without sin among
> you, let him first cast a stone at her. (John 8:6–
> 7)

> Tell us therefore, What thinkest thou? Is it law-
> ful to give tribute unto Caesar or not? But Jesus
> perceived their wickedness, and said, Why
> tempt ye me, ye hypocrites? Shew me the tribute
> money. And they brought unto him a penny.
> And he saith unto them, Whose is this image
> and superscription? They say unto him,
> Caesar's. Then saith he unto them, Render

therefore unto Caesar the things which are Caesar's; and unto God the things that are God's. (Matthew 22:17–21)

Ye shall know them by their fruits. Do men gather grapes of thorns, or figs of thistles? (Matthew 7:16)

Ye are the salt of the earth; but if the salt have lost his savour, wherewith shall it be salted? It is thenceforth good for nothing, but to be cast out, and to be trodden under foot of men. (Matthew 5:13)

These words, so often quoted and recited that one might think them flat and stale, are as alive as ever.

But it would be a mistake to look upon the Gospels as being only books of wisdom in the manner of a Taoist or Confucian text. They are also an account of an historical event – rather obscure, since it was ignored by the historians of the time – which has so deeply affected human beings that one does not know any more whether this historical account is an immense myth, or whether, as some would have it, this myth took the form of a story told from generation to generation for the last two thousand years, and is still commemorated in churches and public squares as a sacred drama.

The scenario has not changed down the years, but each century tells it in its own way so that the myth has become a mirror.

Thus the nineteenth century kept only the compassion, the tenderness and the non-violence of Jesus,
the central figure. That is how Renan* sees it, for
example. Nowadays if Jesus's features are accentuat-
ed it is to put him at the head of all the rebels
throughout the ages and to enlist him in the defence
of the oppressed classes; in short to make him do
battle with Caesar on Caesar's own ground. It is still
Saint Sulpice, but upside down. Thus he is 'taken
over' by politics.[9]

But the essence of the story – what makes it unforgettable – is the infamy of a just man being tor-
tured by a conspiracy of unconscious forces, abandoned, humiliated, crucified, dying upon the cross,
and then, on the third day, came the triumph of life,
the news 'Christ is risen', which spread with incre-
dible speed throughout the Graeco-Roman world
and beyond.

Gurdjieff did not often raise this question of
Christianity. He considered we had no knowledge at
all in this field.

'Imagine', he said, 'that an educated European,
*that is to say a man who knows nothing about
religion*, comes across the possibility of following a religious way. He will see nothing. . .' etc.,
etc.

* Ernest Renan (1825–92) the French scientist and professor
whose thinking dominated the middle of the nineteenth century.
His *Vie de Jésus* in particular exerted a profound influence.

When Ouspensky asked Gurdjieff: 'What is the relation of the teaching you are expounding to Christianity as we know it?' He answered: 'I do not know what you know about Christianity. It would be necessary to talk for a long time, in order to make clear what you understand by this term. But for the benefit of those who know already I will say that, if you like, this is esoteric Christianity.'[10]

Gurdjieff used these words when speaking to pupils who can be called 'Christians' (with all the limitations implicit in this term), since they belonged to pre-Revolutionary Russia, and since their personal search had led them either to try to free themselves from an influence which had disappointed them, or instead to explore its mysteries in order to rediscover its essential meaning.

He once said to pupils who had come from England and the United States to join him at the Prieuré at Avon, that only the man who is able to put Christ's commandments *into practice* can be called a Christian. Referring to the well-known commandment to love one's neighbour as oneself, he asked who was able to do this? 'If you have had a cup of coffee, you love; if not, you do not love.'

'Dr X, if you are struck on the right cheek will you offer the left one?'

The commandments exist as an ideal, but the knowledge that would enable us to keep them is lost. However, such knowledge constitutes the other half of Christianity, its esotericism. It has been preserved in certain schools. Each one of you will be able to initiate himself into it while staying at the Institute which has been opened at the Prieuré, *on the condition that you feel the need for it.*[11]

Thus he spoke about Christianity only to people who already had some idea of its meaning.

But labels, as we know, mattered little to him. Jewish, Christian, Buddhist, Lamaist, Muslim . . . as soon as one gets to the heart of the matter, whatever the differing names, one comes upon the same truth.

He had already explained these things to his Moscow pupils in 1916, and here we have Ouspensky's very precise account.

'You must understand', he said, 'that every real religion, that is, one that has been created by learned people for a definite aim, consists of two parts. One part teaches *what* is to be done. This part becomes common knowledge and in the course of time is distorted and departs from the original. The other part teaches *how* to do what the first part teaches. This part is preserved in secret in special schools and with its help it is always possible to rectify what has been distorted in the first part or to restore it to what has been forgotten.

Without this second part there can be no

knowledge or religion or in any case such knowledge would be incomplete and very subjective.

This secret part exists in Christianity as well as in other religions and it teaches *how* to carry out the precepts of Christ and what they really mean.'[12]

What is the fundamental sound which emerges from words like these?

Blessed is he who has a soul. Blessed is he who has none, but woe to him who has it in embryo.

Today exists to repair yesterday and to prepare for tomorrow.

Those who have not sown anything during their responsible life will have nothing to reap in the future.

All life is a representation of God. He who sees the representation will see what is represented . . . He who does not love life does not love God.[13]

How often he voiced the idea that there are only two ways of freeing the man (not yet born) from the animal (who carried the man in embryo): *conscious labour* and *suffering voluntarily undertaken*.

This was the Alpha and the Omega of his teaching,

his final message, the bottle which he cast upon the waters, before disappearing into the ocean.

One would have to be deaf and blind not to recognize that this thought and the Christian tradition are identical in essence.

When I speak of a 'virile version' of the Gospels it must be remembered that I was born almost seventy-five years ago into the French Protestant bourgeoisie.

At that time, when the characteristics of the nineteenth century were exaggerated to the point of travesty, science was seen as objective, pitiless, in a word, masculine; whereas religion was subjective, sentimental, tender-hearted, in a word, feminine. These two points of view, at times considered complementary, at times incompatible, formed the basis of the masculine-feminine dialogue. I well remember that among themselves men spoke about religion rather ironically as being a concession to the weakness of women. Only at funerals did they put their pride in their pockets.

Nowadays, however, one could just as easily argue the opposite. Belief in science, like political militancy, is based on the idea of unlimited progress, promising discoveries or marvellous achievements. It generates an often fanatical devotion which is more feminine than masculine. Whereas the metaphysical disquiet which underlies religion requires the courage to open one's eyes unflinchingly to seemingly unanswerable problems, an attitude I would call essentially virile.

In Judaism, and in Islam, religion (without being the particular prerogative of either sex) is primarily a matter for the men. The same is true of early Christianity, whether it be Judaic or Greek.

> Simon Peter said to them: Let Mariham go away from us. For Women are not worthy of life. Jesus said: Lo, I will draw her so that I will make her a man so that she too may become a living spirit which is like you men; for every woman who makes herself a man will enter into the Kingdom of Heaven.[14]

Certain stories suggest that Gurdjieff did not speak kindly of the clergy. Yet how could a profoundly religious man not feel an instinctive estrangement from Church officials? The best known example which at once springs to mind is Jesus of Nazareth who, having clashed all his life with the formalism of the Pharisees – that 'race of vipers' and 'whited sepulchres', as he called them – was finally delivered to his executioners by the High Priest himself!

Gurdjieff's anti-clericalism was not only directed against Pope, Archimandrite or Patriarch but also against priests of other confessions, whether disguised as laymen or not. He included in it our ultimate fantasy when he spoke of 'your Mister God' (a character tailored to our own image, who, while strolling in his garden, takes cigars from his pockets and offers them to the chosen, as he did in the film *Green Pastures*).

None of us will ever forget Mr Gurdjieff's funeral service, which took place with great ceremony in the Russian cathedral in the rue Daru in Paris. I do not think that the clergymen who officiated on that day will readily forget it either. So great was the attentiveness it was as if a mass of flames rose above the coffin. The congregation stood, as it does in all Orthodox Church services, and remained absolutely silent, refusing to depart until long after the last lights had been put out and the door of the iconostasis closed.

Where did Gurdjieff come from? We know nothing about his childhood or the town of Kars where he was born. The province of Kars, formerly populated by Greeks and Armenians, had been annexed by Russia a few years after his birth. Moving with the great wave of Western technology which the Russian Empire represented at the time, with its telegraph, railways and administrators, and then outdistancing it, he penetrated into the heart of central Asia in search of monasteries and other places where secret knowledge was preserved. He never spoke to us about this period of his life.

From the time he reappeared in Russia (which was still Holy Tsarist Russia) his peregrinations from East to West are better known to us. It is difficult to say whether these were due to circumstances or to fate, or whether they are proof that he had undertaken a mission to the West.

In Paris, where he settled, he was part of the first big influx of exiles from Russia. The Prieuré at Avon, near Fontainebleau, which he bought in 1924, in order to open his *Institute for the Harmonious Development of Man*, is history (so close to us that we can almost touch it), but it is also legend since we only know of the life there through the extraordinary stories told by those who experienced it.

It is worthy of note that Gurdjieff's move to the West did not end in France, a mere western cape of Europe; nor in the 'valiant little island off the coast of France', as a journalist humorously described Great Britain when we were all but erased from the map of the 'free world' and England stood alone against the might of the Axis.

He visited the United States several times, wanting to make sure before he died that his teaching was firmly planted there.

Where did Gurdjieff come from or, rather, from where was he returning? From exile, a long exile which he could not be said to have submitted to, since he had given it a meaning and had voluntarily taken all the consequences upon himself. Seen in this light his solemn funeral service, celebrated according to the rites of the Russian Orthodox Church, signified the return of an exile to the land of his birth. It restored him to the motherly arms of the Church in the presence of his two families joined anew, the one of the blood, the other of the spirit.

However ignorant we may have been of the liturgical language used in the Orthodox service, we could recognize the 'Gospeli pomeloi' and the 'Kyrie eleison', phrases which had comforted all his ancestors.

It is true that we are all exiles, for when we enter this world we are banished from the unknown country of our arising. As we leave childhood behind we feel ourselves being driven from its verdant paradise. And in the end we shall still cling to the last remaining threads of life, instead of preparing for the inevitable.

Now one of Mr Gurdjieff's characteristics was that he never regretted the past. The high plateaux of Anatolia, the stupas of Buddhist Asia, the gilded cupolas of Russian churches, even the vulgar hubbub of Broadway? They were all one to him. Being everywhere in exile, he was everywhere at home.

In the rue des Acacias in Paris there is a bistro which I never pass without glancing inside, because many a time I saw Mr Gurdjieff sitting there, on a red moleskin-covered bench, studying the customers at the bar as they enacted the human comedy which, though endlessly renewed, is always the same. To behold Mr Gurdjieff for an instant without being seen by him was so exceptional that I have never forgotten it. I remember that his face, the face of an old athlete imbued with compassion for human beings, had an air of melancholy about it, as if he belonged already to an 'elsewhere' which he would not name.

This was during the last years of his life.

The essentially Christian flavour of the teaching, so rightly called 'unknown' by Ouspensky, generally passes unnoticed. That Gurdjieff wished it to be so is beyond doubt. If he had revealed to us that he was teaching in the direct line of the Gospels – which is what emerges for us from the reading of his books – he would have caused the worst kind of misunderstandings. We were not *ripe* for such a confidence.

Our discernment on this particular point went no further than that of the cow in the story he loved to tell. This cow, well cared for by her owner, went out each day into the fields, and in the evening would return to her stall by herself, without anyone having to show her the way. Without ever making a mistake, she used to stop in front of her door, push it open, go in and find her bedding and her manger. One day, however, it so happened that she stopped at a door which seemed to be *her* door and yet she did not recognize it, for during the day someone had painted it red.

Gurdjieff was irresistible when he described the cow, torn between 'Yes, that's definitely my stall' and 'No, it can't possibly be!' The cow's perplexity, the thickness of her bulk pierced by a gleam of awareness, became our own concern because the animal in the fable represents man.

In order to evoke this situation he used the tone of voice at once mocking and indulgent which we also heard whenever he called somebody a *svolatch*, a Russian word for scoundrel. For men and animals each have their own place on the great scale which links all living creatures.

Who thought of painting the door red? That is a question better not asked. However, I like to recall here Luther at the dawn of the Reformation nailing his theses to the closed door of the church at Wittenberg, or, in our time, Gurdjieff, behind a Tantric mask, making his way towards the West after two thousand years of Christianity.

It was Paul Valéry who said: 'To think is to lose the thread.' A surprising statement, you may say. But what he meant was real thought, capable of questioning, and not the thoughts which flow with the current, by the association of ideas, as soon as active and fervent questioning ceases in our minds.[15]

I am not trying to establish without further discussion that Gurdjieff was Christian. I refuse to think like a computer only in terms of 'yes' or 'no'. The question whether or not Gurdjieff was Christian (or whether at one and the same time he was and was not) is much too important to be dismissed superficially.

For the crisis in which we are all involved on the planet Earth, and which shakes the very foundations of our existence and our civilization, is the ending of Christianity.

Could it be that a new bud is sprouting on the old Christian tree in front of our eyes?

In order to be certain that this is so perhaps we need to recall the dogmas of the Revelation, the Incarnation, the Holy Trinity, the Redemption, the Communion of Saints and the Resurrection of the Body and, removing them from the museums where they have been stored, to examine these solemn devices – this, of course, with the help of theologians – in order to re-establish them in the fullness of their meaning and to compare them with the electrifying affirmations which correspond to them in the teachings of Gurdjieff.

But this would be going far beyond the promise I made myself to say only two or three essential things about Mr Gurdjieff.

As an example of the non-dogmatic and entirely practical way in which he taught I will describe what happened to me one Christmas Eve (the Russian Christmas which is thirteen days later than ours). I had been asked to go to his flat where I found another of his pupils. The master of the house showed us into the empty drawing-room, and there in the middle of the floor lay piles of toys, sweetmeats and oranges. We had to divide them up and put them into little paper bags, so that each child could have his share.

A lovely pine tree, fresh from the flower market, confirmed that everything would be done according to custom. I took it upon myself to transform it into a Christmas tree with the necessary tinsel, candles and stars. For someone from Alsace, like myself, this was a deeply satisfying task.

I had almost finished when Mr Gurdjieff came in, glanced at our work, and going up to the tree signalled to me to hang it from the ceiling. I could not believe my eyes. 'But ... Monsieur ... from that hook up there? Upside down, with the roots in the air?' That was exactly what he wanted. So, I was left to strip the tree, climb on a stool and attach the roots to the ceiling as best I could. As for the candles I had no instructions and Mr Gurdjieff had already left the room.

The story is perplexing. It is easy to say: 'This man has his own way of doing things. Stop wondering about him.' On the contrary, I always ascribe to him a precise intention in everything he did. What was the intention in that instance? He who has ears to hear let him hear!

Although we might tend to accept it or reject it completely, following our natural inclination to laziness, Gurdjieff's teaching cannot be so cheaply manipulated! Its invigorating and provoking quality is inexhaustible.

I will give you two examples of this. The first one does not seem at first sight to be connected with the biblical or Christian dogmas just mentioned. I am referring to *Beelzebub's Tales to His Grandson*. What is the main thread running through it? It is the exile of Beelzebub, who was banished from the planet of his birth for a sin which he had committed out of excess of pride in his youth. Thereafter, in the course of a long journey which took him to the utmost confines of the solar system, he was obliged to undergo a series of trials in order to acquire the experience and wisdom he lacked. Here one recognizes the scenario (journey – ordeals – achievement) common to voyages of initiation in all traditions. A Christian would call it a story of redemption.

Gurdjieff's challenge consists in choosing as hero of this adventure the Prince of Darkness himself, that is to say Beelzebub, as if to remind us that evil is not excluded from the laws of the universe, but is, on the contrary, and at all levels, one of its mainsprings, the principle without which there could be no individual redemption.

This question will not leave us in peace.

The second example touches us Christians particularly, for it concerns a certain person, Judas, whom from childhood we have been taught to consider as the arch-traitor of all time.

He handed over his master. He collected the reward for his betrayal, his thirty pieces of silver. And then he went and hanged himself. Shame and damnation be upon him forever!

Now, in *Beelzebub's Tales*, Gurdjieff tells the story differently. Judas, he says, was the best and most faithful of all the disciples. Jesus, who saw him every day until the fatal Last Supper could not have failed to discern the innermost thoughts of his disciple's heart. If we read the scene of the arrest in the Gospels we can be sure that, in fact, the two principal actors, Jesus and Judas, were acting in perfect connivance. Iscariot had been charged with the worst possible mission: to appear to betray his master. He acquitted himself with great courage. How then can one explain the fact that for two thousand years Christianity has unceasingly cursed the name of Judas? Here I take the liberty of pointing out that throughout history Christianity has likewise cursed the Jewish people, accusing it of 'deicide' and holding it responsible for the death of Christ. Only after a decision of Vatican II was this fantastic accusation withdrawn.[16]

During the meetings that Gurdjieff had with his pupils in Moscow or St Petersburg in 1916, he explained how the Christian Church as we know it came into being, and what its true function originally was.

Here is a long extract from this important text:

> We know very little about Christianity and the form of Christian worship; we know nothing at all of the history and origin of a number of things. For instance, the church, the temple in which gather the faithful and in which services are carried out according to specific rites; where was this taken from? Many people do not think about this at all. Many people think that the

outward form of worship, the rites, the singing of canticles, and so on, were invented by the fathers of the church. Others think that this outward form has been taken partly from pagan religions and partly from the Hebrews. But all this is untrue. The question of the origin of the Christian church, that is, of the Christian temple, is more interesting than we think. To begin with, the church and worship in the form which they took in the first centuries of Christianity could not have been borrowed from paganism because there was nothing like it either in the Greek or Roman cults or in Judaism. The Jewish synagogue, the Jewish temple, the Greek and Roman temples of various gods, were something quite different from the Christian church which made its appearance in the first and second centuries. The Christian church is a school concerning which people have forgotten that it is a school. Imagine a school where the teachers give lectures and perform explanatory demonstrations for ceremonies, or rites, or 'sacraments', i.e. magic. This would approximate to the Christian church of our times.

The Christian church, the Christian form of worship, was not invented by the fathers of the church. It was all taken in a ready-made form from Egypt, only not from the Egypt that we know but from one which we do not know.

This Egypt was in the same place as the other but it existed much earlier. Only small bits of it survived in historical times, and these bits have been preserved in secret and so well that we do not even know where they have been preserved.

It will seem strange to many people when I say that this pre-historic Egypt was Christian many thousands of years before the birth of Christ, that is to say, that its religion was composed of the same principles and ideas that constitute true Christianity. Special schools existed in this pre-historic Egypt which were called 'schools of repetition'. In these schools a public repetition was given on definite days, and in some schools perhaps even every day, of the entire course in a condensed form of the sciences that could be learned at these schools. Sometimes this repetition lasted a week or a month. Thanks to these repetitions people who had passed through this course did not lose their connection with the school and retained in their memory all they had learned. Sometimes they came from very far away simply in order to listen to the repetition and went away feeling their connection with the school. There were special days of the year when the repetitions were particularly complete, when they were carried out with particular solemnity –

51

and these days themselves possessed a symbolical meaning.

These 'schools of repetition' were taken as a model for Christian churches – the form of worship in Christian churches almost entirely represents the course of repetition of the science dealing with the universe and man. Individual prayers, hymns, responses, all had their own meaning in this repetition as well as holidays and all religious symbols, though their meaning has been forgotten long ago.

And further on he adds:

A ceremony is a book in which a great deal is written. Anyone who understands can read it. One rite often contains more than a hundred books.[17]

In the light of this reply we discover the profoundly traditional aspect of Gurdjieff's thought. This is only a step away from enlisting him in the traditionalist camp, among those who by taking Western thought to extremes consider, in the name of the one and only primordial tradition, that progress is a delusion.

Likewise, if we choose to consider only one aspect of his thought we could see him as one of the inspirers of the ecological movement, or even as a forerunner of psychoanalysis.

Gurdjieff appeared at the beginning of this century like a megalith, a survivor of some unknown catastrophe, set there as a challenge in his isolation: in a word, he was an anachronism.

This is no longer so. Under the pressure of all the archaeological, ethnological, psychoanalytical and sociological discoveries which challenge once more the unduly narrow views of the nineteenth century, our century has caught up with him, and is even trying to appropriate him. Faced with this phenomenon, which is especially evident on the West Coast of America, in California, I feel like asking: 'How will they serve him up next?'

But let us return to traditionalism. This word took on a quite different meaning in the 1950s and its current (non-philosophical) sense is quasi-synonymous with conformism and conservatism. This is its debased meaning. Etymologically (from the Latin *tradere*: to transmit) the emphasis must be put on the transmission of a living primordial knowledge and not at all on a blind attachment to the forms and structures of the past.

In Orthodox Church services there is a perfect symbolical representation of tradition every time a member of the congregation holds a candle and lights it from his neighbour's flame. This little flame – which the slightest breath could blow out – is, in fact, fire – fire coming from another fire which, passing from one person to the next, will light as many flames as there are souls present. The image is perfect because fire, reborn from fire, cannot be corrupted.

But is anything incorruptible in the current of life?

As Gurdjieff explains elsewhere, nothing can ever remain still, everything that does not ascend is destined to descend. The higher the source the deeper the descent. Religious teachings are no exception. He once explained this in a very picturesque way when answering one of his Moscow pupils. He was asked if one could find 'anything real in the teaching and rituals of existing religions, or anything that might lead one to attain something real'.

> 'Yes and no', said G. 'Imagine that we are sitting here talking of religions and that the maid Masha hears our conversation. She, of course, understands it in her own way and she repeats what she has understood to the porter Ivan. The porter Ivan again understands it in his own way and he repeats what he has understood to the coachman Peter next door. The coachman Peter goes to the country and recounts in the village what the gentry talk about in town. Do you think what he recounts will at all resemble what we said? This is precisely the relation between existing religions and that which was their basis. You get teachings, traditions, prayers, rites, not at fifth but at twenty-fifth hand, and, of course, almost everything has been distorted beyond recognition and everything essential forgotten long ago.'[18]

This short fable, by the way, also illustrates the debasement that Gurdjieff's teaching may undergo in the future. If one tries to turn it into a doctrine in order to preserve it intact, it will cease to be a leaven.

But let us return to the text concerning the origins of the Church. Christianity is not confined to the historical and geographical bounds of the New Testament, nor even to the much larger framework of the Bible. Its roots lie buried in ancient Egypt – 'presand Egypt' as it is called by the author of *Meetings with Remarkable Men*. Beyond this unknown Egypt it is embedded in the civilizations which may have existed on earth before the great perturbations described in *Beelzebub's Tales to His Grandson*. Total though this disaster was, it has, however, always been possible for those who were about to disappear to leave certain traces for those who come after to find.

A rising sap, secret and unique, animated all civilizations prior to our own. The oldest tree that has ever grown on this earth can thus be called by the name of one of its main branches: Christianity. If one of these branches withers it will grow green again elsewhere. This is a wager we are always ready to make. 'We civilizations now know that we are mortal' is a warning that we heard when we were young.[19] But it is in the very nature of man to begin his stubborn and apparently useless effort over and over again in order to attain the unattainable: he will always take up a challenge.

According to the text just quoted, the challenge for the early Christians was to keep alive certain revealed

55

truths, in spite of the inertia and death which always threatened them.

A truth is revealed in fact like a legacy entrusted to man. Man is responsible for the spark of consciousness which he alone has received out of all the creatures who inhabit the earth. This puts him in great peril, in danger as he is of yielding to the lulling charms of nature – his own nature – the moment he ceases to use those faculties which alone distinguish him from animals and plants. He is required, and endlessly reminded, to *watch*.

A fully awakened man will not be completely dependent on surrounding influences, nor entirely taken in by appearances, since he will be able to distinguish the essence from the form which contains it. He will maintain the form as long as it envelops the essence; but he will not attach himself to it, and will even know how to break out of it.

Let René Guénon conclude:

> Metaphysical truth is eternal. By the same token there have always been those who have been able to know it truly and totally. Outer forms and contingent ways may change but there is nothing in this very change which belongs to what is nowadays called *evolution*. It is merely a simple adaptation to this or that particular circumstance, to conditions specific to a race and to a given epoch.[20]

Was Gurdjieff a traditionalist? It would be much

more correct to say that everything about him was traditional: *he was himself the tradition.*

Many a time on the journeys some of us have made to Morocco, Afghanistan, Tibet and India, we have imagined ourselves coming across him on a street corner or in a bar at the heart of some bazaar!

Gurdjieff enjoyed embellishing his words and writings with spicy but scathing aphorisms and proverbs, which he attributed to Mullah Nassr Eddin, the legendary character who brings to life the popular wisdom of Asia. It is strange that the only traditional authority, under the cover of which he introduced himself into Europe, was this unknown figure. However much the scholars rummage through libraries and pore over manuscripts, they will not find anything which can be attributed to Mullah Nassr Eddin – and with good reason!

There is no doubt that Gurdjieff wanted to cover the tracks of his past, to conceal the name of the chain of tradition, or initiation of which he was the culmination. This has always made him suspect in the eyes of the traditionalists; I mean those who did not possess, besides other necessary qualities, the sense of humour indispensable for 'scenting', even from afar, his allegiance to tradition.

Herein lies a mystery. He was a profoundly religious man, so traditional that, having known him, we can open any one of the sacred texts of mankind and perceive their meaning as if he had given us the key. Yet such a man introduces himself to the West behind an anti-traditional mask! Given that I do not use these words in their geographical sense only, I believe that the whole question of the relationship between East and West is outlined in this pheno-menon.

The West, which is in the process of invading the whole planet, seems *to have reached the point of no return*. Nations reputed to be traditional are dragged irrevocably in its wake. In Mao's China bulldozers obliterate all traces of the ancestors' tombstones; Nigeria buys factories to produce atomic bombs; nowadays machine gun fire can be heard around the city of Nazareth.[21]

A movement of such breadth cannot be withstood. It probably answers a cosmic need which is beyond us. No return to the source of the Nile, nor to the source of the Ganges; no ascent of Mount Meru, no expedition to New Guinea; no plunging into the depths of a volcano will help us to discover the treasure of lost knowledge which from now on is no longer behind us, but ahead of us, in us. Nothing will prevent men from turning towards the unknown within themselves and from going through a thou-sand ordeals towards this unknown, stored, accord-ing to Gurdjieff, like a treasure *intact* in the depths of their own unconscious.

I had hardly finished writing these pages; I had hardly put them down before reading them over and com-pleting them with any notes that might prove necessary, when I suddenly asked myself: 'Have I not attempted the impossible?'

'And for you,' I feel like asking my friends, craftily edging my manuscript towards them, 'who is he for you?' But I know that every one of those who met him would, if asked, give a picture of his own, different from that of his neighbour. For each one looked at him differently, each heard him with his own subjectivity.

I remember a misadventure which many years ago befell a promising young writer, who was interested in the teaching of Gurdjieff as a method of self-development. He had never met the master. One day, however, the encounter almost took place. The young man saw the redoubtable silhouette in the distance (it was in the corridors of the Salle Pleyel) and immediately projected onto this image his ancestral fear of the bogeyman, which was no doubt waiting for just this moment to materialize. He then undertook to write a book over five-hundred pages long on *Monsieur Gurdjieff*, warning the prospective reader 'that, in order to produce this book, he had had to act as compiler, journalist and detective'.

I wonder what we would know about Pythagoras or Heraclitus, Socrates or Jesus, had we discovered police records concerning them in the archives of the time. Why not laundry lists or Metro tickets? These, together with newspaper articles and other 'material proof', make up the 'objective' elements of information that historians devote themselves to collecting if they have nothing else to get their teeth into.

I would say that Gurdjieff cannot be taken as an *object* of knowledge for he is, *par excellence*, a *subject*. In my view no real knowledge, and I venture to say no objective knowledge, is possible if one contents oneself with the testimony of others. One must enter, as Gurdjieff invites us to do, into a personal relationship with him, whatever the cost and whatever the difficulty. But is not a personal relationship by its very nature incommunicable?

To answer this question I would conclude that my testimony, like all writings of the kind which aspire to convey a life, are merely literary exercises – 'titillations', as Gurdjieff would have said.

Had I allowed such doubts to cross my mind while writing, I would very soon have abandoned the attempt and I would not have had to empty my waste-paper basket so many times.

But 'God knows more!' say the Muslims, at the end of any discussion, in order not to be caught in the trap of deadly dialectic.

There is food for thought in the fly's insistent beating against the same window-pane when the way out and freedom are actually behind it. The ancients were much impressed by the fact that the sun itself, whose royalty and inexhaustible energy are incontestable, borrowed the circling of the moon at night in order to affirm its own permanence.

With Gurdjieff we learnt that a straight line is not

always the shortest distance from one point to another.

But I do not wish to move on now to something which will be developed later. Rather let us ask ourselves what should be the nature of an eye capable of seeing through appearances, which are always in movement, always subjective, in order to open a door to what is the aim of all true knowledge: objectivity.

There is no doubt that the capacity for such looking exists. I see proof of this in the miracle of painting. Some painters have known how to look at the reality which surrounds us with such freshness of vision that it is as if the skies had suddenly opened and another light was shining, unfolding before us the splendour which is nearly always hidden by the thick crust of habit.

I look at Delft as Vermeer saw it and *I see Delft*.

It could be said that this extraordinary phenomenon is simply due to the painter's skill. I do not deny that this is one factor in the miracle. But virtuosity alone has never made great music or great painting. Renoir worked till the end of his life, wearing splints on his arms that were crippled with rheumatism. Illness had neither blurred nor deposed his abiding child-like vision.

This is indeed the first and indispensable quality needed to approach Gurdjieff: innocence – the innocence of the little boy who exclaims as the procession passes by, 'the Emperor has no clothes!' It exists at any age. This little patch of childhood that remains intact in spite of all the ills of life, in spite of 'education', is pure gold, the trace of gold without which, as alchemists know, no gold can be made.

If Gurdjieff gave anything to a child, even a raisin, the mother would hastily prompt him with 'What do you say?' Silence. The mother would keep on until the child would finally say in a small mechanical voice, 'Thank you.' Then, like a thief caught red-handed, the mother would hear words vibrant with anger raining down upon her. 'You, mother, you shit on source from where real feelings will arise later . . . you spoil all future. . . .'

It was a joy to see children take their place at Mr Gurdjieff's table, sitting like grown-ups with their parents. It did not take them long to enter the dance; I mean that yielding to his subtle provocation, they engaged without the slightest reservation in the playful or dialectic activity which the master invented to suit their measure.

We, the 'grown-ups' were subjected to similar provocations which, I must say, were difficult to resist. For, with his truly fiendish attention to practicalities, Gurdjieff perceived each one of our inner movements and modified his game, depending on whether we went forward or back.

Out of wariness we often clung to our position of simple spectators. For children, however, the reverse is true: anything they have not yet experienced is irresistible. That is why games attract them.

A game is 'serious activity *par excellence*, for no-one can contest its rules'.[22] It requires the player's whole-hearted participation. 'Are you playing or not?' At the end of the game, however, I will not die: the rules of the game will be abolished. Another rule, more important and more difficult to decipher, will establish its prerogative once again.

The spark of mischief which gleams in the eyes of a small child at the idea of a game, the challenge which shines in the eyes of the athlete before a contest, the unshakable calm behind which the chess-player hides his next move, express, in spite of appearances, the same resolution.

I would willingly uphold that there is only one game, the archetypal game of which all the others, regardless of the real or apparent diversity of their rules, are just variations.

This game could be formulated thus: try (to win). Just as you are, here, immediately, take stock of yourself, discover who you are.

The newborn child, in the first few moments when he lies, all unseeing, in his mother's arms, does not question anything yet. As soon as he opens his eyes he will begin to do so. Since everything ends in suffering, decay, and finally death, to shut him up in a sheep-pen, behind the thick walls of reassuring ideologies, would only serve to deceive him. Let him rather hear the tigers that are always prowling outside those walls. They at least are real.

If the innocent escapes the 'massacre of the innocents' or, in other words, the bludgeoning of virtue by vice, if he keeps his heart pure in spite of the wickedness, deceit and violence which hold sway in this world, he will be given as a counterweapon the magic word, the cunning, thanks to which he will triumph. The Bible, the *Thousand and One Nights*, fables, legends, fairy tales and myths (from Tierra del Fuego to Alaska) abound with stories of this kind. The forces of evil are destroyed or reduced to slavery by the patience and *slyness* of the weakest.

This is why Gurdjieff once called his teaching the *way of the sly man*.

I believe he cared too much for human beings to dupe them with the promise of 'entering heaven with their boots on'. His slyness was directed against all forms of what he calls 'auto-satisfaction', in particular against that of the man who, having found a guru, falls in behind him, ceases all effort and abandons the use of any critical faculty.

He came to waken man, if it is not too late, by reminding him of his dignity – not to anaesthetize him.

Some people saw him as Merlin the Magician, others as the Devil, and these are only two of the many aspects of himself that he was able to present.

In order to meet his eye one would have needed both the candid, defenceless gaze of the newborn babe and the keen eye of the hunter alone in the bush, who is attentive to the slightest sign.

Was he our partner in the game? Or was he a rule, as yet unknown, of the game he embodied – a rule which would be revealed to us only in the act of playing?

I am not sure that my thought is sufficiently clear.

Another expression which may mean more to some people than 'the rules of the game' is 'the trueness of the game' in the sense that one says that a musician plays true.

It is obvious that the game Gurdjieff was playing in the comical, absurd, odious or ridiculous situations in which he sometimes placed his pupils was one of extreme rigour. And in this game, into which he voluntarily allowed himself to be drawn, he always *played true*.

'All right, then,' but in the end the reader may say, eager to know my conclusions, 'in the end did you meet the real Gurdjieff?'

Who could pride himself on ever having met Gurdjieff?

A master meets you for the sole purpose of showing you the direction, the way to the inner master which is called conscience. He helps you to discover that you are already its subject, but that you were not aware of it.

And then he disappears. He melts into the sky as the mountain does the moment you believe you have set foot on it.

Addendum

Addendum

In spite of their shortcomings I offer these lines to
the public to indicate the place of a deeper debate
which others will one day feel to be necessary and
even urgent. It is like putting a buoy in the water to
show that on the seabed there lies a wreck, a danger-
spot or a treasure.

P.12 '. . . because the spectacle which followed the
various toasts drunk to "the idiots" was
extraordinary.'

Unless accompanied by the appropriate commentary, 'spectacle' is the word least applicable to the
meals which Mr Gurdjieff invited us to every week.
They were feasts that demanded one's complete participation, banquets for body, heart and mind.

Eating is, in itself, a sacred act, since it serves to
sustain life. Every time men sit round a table to eat
and drink together they celebrate life, but usually
they are only dimly aware of it.

The wedding feasts in Brittany, as described by
Pierre Jakez Helias in *Cheval d'Orgueil* may, perhaps, give a foretaste of what we were privileged to
experience on Thursday evenings in the rue des Co-
lonels Renard.

The setting, however, was far from grand; an
ordinary bourgeois dining room too small to hold us

all, and whose ill-assorted chairs could have come from any saleroom.

Mr Gurdjieff would have sitting next to him someone he had publicly designated as 'director' or 'tamada' of the meal, and who would be one of us. This person dispensed the alcohol, and gave the toasts, one after the other, at the right moment, in words which demanded great exactness. Our glasses, filled with vodka or armagnac, stood before us untouched until the first toast.

Then the *tamada* stood up, and announced with the assurance of *marabout*: 'To the health of all ordinary idiots . . .' After which, turning to the fellow-guests he knew to be 'ordinary idiots', he greeted them by their name (or nickname), '. . . and to your health, your Honour', '. . . and to your health too, Doctor', 'and to your health too, Miss X'. We would put down our glasses only after downing the contents at one gulp.

When the clatter of spoons and forks resumed, the generous alcohol was already working in us, and adding with the tasty food to the indefinable but profound impression we experienced on hearing our comrades addressed by the title which defined their true status.

The next toast was 'to the health of all superior idiots'. If there were any idiots of this kind at the table the *tamada* would now turn to each one of them. 'And to your health, so and so . . . ', 'and to your health also, sir . . .' And so on. Later we would

70

drink to the 'arch-idiots', 'hopeless idiots', 'round idiots', 'square idiots', 'zig-zag idiots' and others, without ever reaching the ultimate degrees of this hierarchy. For me they remain a mystery. Some, fearing the effects of the alcohol, began to cheat immediately after the second or third glass, having first ensured the complicity of the *tamada* and, perhaps the tacit agreement of Mr Gurdjieff who, I am sure, missed nothing of what went on at that table.

Some say that for Gurdjieff there were twenty-one categories of idiot ranging in 'degrees of reason' from the reason of an ordinary man up to the reason of our All-Embracing Endlessness, God, the unique idiot. Others maintain that there were only thirteen.

I never heard him speak on this subject. I shall simply say that to be described as an idiot, which would be taken as an insult if it were thrown in your face by a passing stranger, was vested, in his presence, with an inexplicable grandeur.

The Greek root *idios* means particularity. The entire edifice of idiocity was perhaps merely a wonderful device intended to help us to see in others, and to discover in ourselves, certain particularities so deeply encrusted in our nature that we would have been incapable of discerning them without this artifice: a play of mirrors where others served as reflections of our own image.

The idiots of the first category were, according to the director's commentary: *those who do not take themselves for dog's tail*. Of course, they could not

71

be just shit, could they! But let us not carry the joke too far, for self-esteem, when stung to the quick, can make us turn very nasty.

The next idiots, *those who have five Fridays a week*, consisted of the people, male or female, who display the characteristics of *hysterical women*. They were, in the words of Beelzebub, the 'very resolute, very honoured and certainly very patient gentlemen' as well as the 'very dear, patient and impartial ladies' who waste their energies in a flood of words and disorderly actions.

I myself was one of the 'arch-idiots'. How was one to understand that? Maybe it was only a joke? Someone had once heard Mr Gurdjieff reply, when questioned on this subject: 'Arch? As in architect . . . archdeacon . . . archidiacre. . . .' It was really a joke, then! Yet it stressed a side of my nature which was as unknown to me as my own smell: respect for established hierarchies.

The fourth toast, 'to the health of all the hopeless idiots', was accompanied by a fuller commentary which the *tamada* was bound to repeat, word for word, even if he did not always fathom its deep meaning. It exploded like thunder, leaving no room for any ambiguity, since it was said that among all those 'hopeless idiots' some were *candidates for dying like dogs* and others *candidates for dying honourably*. The distinction was as follows: the first *were without objective hope* (will die like dogs); the second *without subjective hope* (called upon to die honourably). In order to be without subjective hope, he explained further, it is necessary to have worked on oneself during one's life.

These alcoholic libations have been severely criticized by those who have only heard about them without actually taking part. But one must not forget that these ceremonies took place under the master's eye.

I do not know which is more to be admired: that no one ever sank, body and soul, into drunkenness; or that when the glasses and plates had been removed, no two guests ever lacked mutual respect to the point of beginning to speak at the same time in front of Mr Gurdjieff when, like the opening of a sacred duel, the right to put a question to him was given.

P. 52 '. . . we could see him as one of the inspirers of the ecological movement . . .'

It is not betraying Gurdjieff to link him with Pythagoras and the Hermetic tradition. The central idea of this unique tradition which has borne in succession the names of gnosticism, alchemy, etc., is the unity of all living things and, as a result, their mutual dependence.

On this subject Gurdjieff puts these words into the mouth of Mullah Nassr Eddin: *'Better-pull-ten-hairs-a-day-out-of-your-mother's-head-than-not-help-Nature.'* For, as he himself says in *Beelzebub's Tales:* 'this unfortunate Nature of the planet Earth must continuously, and without respite, adapt Herself to manifest otherwise, always otherwise, so as to remain within the common-cosmic harmony.'

Here Gurdjieff shows his sympathy not only for men who, in their ignorance, play the role of stirrers-up of strife, but also for the planet itself, obliged as it is to re-establish the cosmic equilibrium.

This is the 'naturalist' aspect (nowadays one would say the 'ecological' aspect) of the author of *Beelzebub's Tales*. When he describes the great winds that shook the earth, the rising up of mountains, etc., these phenomena are never isolated from their environment, never thought of as abnormal but always as necessary.

For the ecologist the idea that the environment and its inhabitants form a whole, and the idea of Reciprocal Feeding in particular, are both absolutely central. He can verify it daily on the scale of our planet. Enlarged to a gigantic scale it becomes the principle of *Reciprocal Maintenance of All Existing Things* which governs the universe.

P.52 '. . . or even as a forerunner of psychoanalysis . . .'

Gurdjieff knew a great deal about hypnotism. In *Beelzebub's Tales* he rehabilitates the memory of Mesmer and even alludes to the works in which Freud's discoveries had their origins.

But there is little doubt that he had access in his youth to other sources on this subject, sources unknown to our science and probably located in Asia. The care he took to cover their tracks should restrain us from going in search of them.

The real adventure to which he calls any man courageous enough to attempt it is that of daring to look down into the abyss of his own unconscious. Can we, like Theseus, enter our inner labyrinth, at the risk of never meeting the Minotaur, of never seeing daylight again, deceived by an infernal game of echoes and false exits as in a never-ending course of psychoanalysis?

The 'who am I?', the act, the question which Gurdjieff urged his disciples to renew as often as possible, seems to me to be the Ariadne's thread of this other adventure. The day when, explained the master, if God pleases, you meet your own ego – look it in the face, challenge it! When it is dead (from having been seen) you will at least be freed.

The first condition for this utterly intimate act is silence and collectedness. It has nothing to do with the 'liberation' which takes place on the psychoanalyst's couch.

Notes

Notes

1 If his passport is to be believed, George Ivanovitch Gurdjieff was born on 28 December 1877 in the town of Alexandropo (now Leninakan in the USSR).

2 Bodhidharma, the Indian monk who brought Buddhism to China, is certainly less well known in our part of the world than he is in the Far East. Let us not forget that he founded a Buddhist esotericism called Ch'an in Chinese, Zen in Japanese, and that there are obvious analogies between this discipline and the method taught to Westerners by Gurdjieff. Painters have represented Bodhidharma as an old man whose piercing gaze cannot be avoided, because it follows you wherever you happen to stand.

3 We know now that one episode of Gurdjieff's youth took place in Crete in 1896 when he joined the ranks of Greek patriots at the time of their rebellion against Turkish domination. It was then that he was wounded 'by a stray bullet'. Obviously I knew nothing about this when I was introduced to Gurdjieff in 1943, but I had travelled, on foot and by mule, through Crete in the summer of 1931 to make a film. In those days the *capetan* were honoured as demi-gods. Survivors of the *maquis*, they looked like authentic brigands and remain engraved in my memory as a pure expression of a Europe which I thought had completely disappeared.

4 '. . . l'effort est d'autant plus grand pour le saisir dans son unité'. Paul Valéry, *Introduction à la Méthode de Leonard de Vinci*, first published in *La Nouvelle Revue*, 15 August 1895.

5 'Le seul homme absolument libre, si cet homme pouvait

79

se concevoir, serait l'homme dont pas un geste ne sentirait l'imitation'. This quotation is from Élie Faure.

6 'Nous finirons par tout savoir et ne rien comprendre.' René Daumal in *La Grande Beuverie* (1933; English translation published in 1980 by Routledge & Kegan Paul), and he adds: 'In no time the schools will know everything about art, without having to create ... know everything about science without having to think about it ... know everything about religion without having to live.'

7 Concerning the three kinds of food received by the human organism cf. *In Search of the Miraculous*, pp. 181 ff.

8 In 1950 *In Search of the Miraculous (Fragments of an Unknown Teaching)* was published by P. D. Ouspensky (Routledge & Kegan Paul). The fruit of eight years of work with Gurdjieff, it was a literary event of considerable importance, since it allowed anyone to acquaint himself with a current of thought that up till then had been available to very few people.

In 1950 *Beelzebub's Tales to His Grandson* appeared in England (Routledge & Kegan Paul); in 1963 *Meetings with Remarkable Men* (Routledge & Kegan Paul). In 1976 *Life is real only then when 'I am'* was published in a private edition. According to Gurdjieff, each of these three very different books answers a specific need, and together they constitute the monumental literary work which he left to posterity. Their collective title is *All and Everything*.

9 The church of Saint Sulpice in Paris towers over a district steeped in Catholicism. When I was young one could buy candles, holy pictures, plaster Virgins and lambs in all the shops in the vicinity. The building itself is of an imposing size, but it is cold and unfriendly and reeks of boredom. The expression 'style Saint Sulpice' can be used to describe all sorts of objects lacking the

spark which would make them real works of art containing a higher meaning.

However much specialists in French history remind us that the 'Sulpiciens' were 'Gallicans' who wanted the Church to keep its distance from the Papacy, for the ordinary people like us Saint Sulpice represents on the contrary what was called 'l'union du sabre et du goupillon', that is to say clericalism seen as having taken sides and supporting both the throne and the altar.

10 *In Search of the Miraculous*, p. 102.
11 *Views from the Real World. Early talks of Gurdjieff, as recollected by his pupils* (Routledge & Kegan Paul), p. 154.
12 *In Search of the Miraculous*, p. 304.
13 The first maxim is one of the aphorisms inscribed on the walls of the Institute for the Harmonious Development of Man at the Prieuré at Avon. The other three remain engraved in the minds of those who heard them at the rue des Colonels-Renard.
14 Taken from *The Secret Sayings of Jesus according to the Gospel of Thomas*, Robert M. Grant with David Noel Freedman with an English translation by W. R. Schoedel (Collins/Fontana, 1960). It must be remembered that this collection probably preceded the canonical Gospels and may have been one of their sources. It was discovered in Upper Egypt in 1945. Cf. on this subject and for the complete quotation, without which the answer attributed to Jesus will be misunderstood, *L'Evangile selon Thomas* (translation and commentaries by Philippe Suarez, Métanoia, 1975).
15 Cf. Heidegger: 'Questioning is the piety of thought.'
16 'Only after a decision of Vatican II was this fantastic accusation withdrawn.' Conciliary decree *Nostra Aetate* promulgated by Pope Paul VI, 28 October 1965.
17 Cf. *In Search of the Miraculous*, pp. 302–3.

18 Cf. *In Search of the Miraculous*, p. 96.
19 'Nous autres, civilisations, nous savons maintenant que nous sommes mortelles.' Paul Valéry's famous sentence in his essay on *La Crise de l'Esprit*, far from stating a commonplace, drew its strength from the striking new evidence arising from the First World War. The weekly review the *Athenaeum*, edited by John Middleton Murry, was the first to publish it, as well as the *Nouvelle Revue Française* (1 August 1919). Cf. Paul Valéry, *Variétés*.
20 René Guénon, *La Métaphysique orientale*, lecture given at the Sorbonne, 17 December 1925.
21 On 30 March 1976 the Transjordanian Arabs had organized demonstrations against the agrarian reform that Jerusalem wanted to impose on them. The repression of the Arabs caused many casualties, both dead and wounded, around Nazareth. This episode now appears insignificant when compared with the savage slaughter that has since taken place between 'Christians' and 'Muslims' in the Lebanon. To be precise the countries which in 1976 declared their intention of buying factories to produce atomic bombs were Bangladesh and Rhodesia, not Nigeria. The crisis of civilization into which we are all being drawn is developing so fast that any topical allusion is immediately overtaken by further events.
22 'A game is "serious activity *par excellence*, for no one can contest its rules".' This quotation is from René Alleau. The metaphysical importance of the game could not have been stated more succinctly.